African-American Heroes

LeBron James

Stephen Feinstein

Enslow Elementary

an imprint of

Enslow Publishers, Inc.

40 Industrial Road
Box 398
Berkeley Heights, NJ 07922
USA

http://www.enslow.com

Words to Know

Cavaliers (cav-uh-LEERS)—The pro basketball team in Cleveland, Ohio.

compete—To take part in a contest.

National Basketball Association (NBA)—The group of professional American basketball teams.

national tournament—A contest in which teams from the same country compete in a series of games.

rookie—A beginner; someone in his first year of playing in the NBA.

scouts—People hired by teams to look for their future players.

Enslow Elementary, an imprint of Enslow Publishers, Inc.

Enslow Elementary® is a registered trademark of Enslow Publishers, Inc.

Library of Congress Cataloging-in-Publication Data
Feinstein, Stephen.
　LeBron James / Stephen Feinstein.
　　p. cm.— (African-American heroes)
　Summary: "Examines the life of National Basketball Association all-star LeBron James, including his childhood, early career in basketball, and his path to the NBA"—Provided by publisher.
　Includes index.
　ISBN-13: 978-0-7660-2898-2
　ISBN-10:　　0-7660-2898-4
　1. James, LeBron—Juvenile literature. 2. Basketball players—United States—Biography—Juvenile literature. I. Title.
　GV884.J36F45 2008
　796.323092—dc22
　[B]　　　　　　　　　　2007041588

Printed in the United States of America

10 9 8 7 6 5 4 3 2 1

To Our Readers: We have done our best to make sure all Internet addresses in this book were active and appropriate when we went to press. However, the author and the publisher have no control over and assume no liability for the material available on those Internet sites or on links to other Web sites. Any comments or suggestions can be sent by e-mail to comments@enslow.com or to the address on the back cover.

♻ Enslow Publishers, Inc., is committed to printing our books on recycled paper. The paper in every book contains 10% to 30% post-consumer waste (PCW). The cover board on the outside of each book contains 100% PCW. Our goal is to do our part to help young people and the environment too!

Illustration Credits: AP/Wide World, pp. 2, 3, 7, 8, 12, 15, 16, 17, 18, 19, 20, 21, 22, back cover; Everett Digital, p. 11; Getty Images, pp. 1, 4, 5; Shutterstock, pp. 3, 6.

Cover Illustration: AP/Wide World.

Contents

Chapter 1

The Toy Basketball Set

LeBron James was born on December 30, 1984, in Akron, Ohio. His mother, Gloria, was sixteen and still in high school. LeBron never knew his father. Gloria and LeBron lived with Gloria's mother, Freda.

When LeBron was eight months old, Gloria started dating Eddie Jackson. When Eddie needed a place to stay, Freda let him live at her house.

LeBron James grew up to be one of America's best basketball players.

On Christmas Eve, 1988, Gloria and Eddie were looking forward to the next day. They had bought a toy basketball set for LeBron, who was almost four. But Christmas Eve turned out to be very sad. Later that night, LeBron's grandmother, Freda, suddenly died. She had been very sick, but nobody else knew.

The next day, Gloria and Eddie gave LeBron his Christmas present. They decided not to tell him about his grandma until after

Christmas. When LeBron saw the basketball and hoop, he went wild. Gloria and Eddie watched in amazement as the little boy ran up to the hoop and dunked the ball.

2 On the Move

After Freda died, life was hard for Gloria and LeBron. They were very poor. They did not have a place of their own to live. Eddie went to live with his aunt. Friends let Gloria and LeBron stay with them.

Gloria James, LeBron's mom.

Eddie Jackson. When LeBron was little, Eddie lived with him and his mom.

Gloria and LeBron had some tough times, but she was always his biggest fan.

When LeBron was five, he and his mother moved seven times in one year. Sometimes they lived in the housing projects, apartment houses for poor people. Sometimes there were gang fights there. Gloria and LeBron were always scared about what was going to happen next.

When LeBron was in the fourth grade, he missed eighty-two days of school. Gloria loved LeBron, but she could not take care of him. So she sent LeBron to live with Frankie Walker and his family.

Frankie was a basketball coach at the community center. LeBron had gone to the center to learn how to play basketball. Frankie taught LeBron new moves. LeBron learned very quickly. He learned how to shoot, how to control the ball, and how to play defense.

The Fab Four

Living with the Walker family made a big difference for LeBron. In the fifth grade, he did not miss a single day of school, and his grades were good. LeBron joined a basketball team called the Shooting Stars. He became close friends with three boys on the team, Dru Joyce, Jr., Sian Cotton, and Willie McGee. The four friends called themselves the Fab Four.

LeBron never missed a basketball practice, and he kept getting better. The Shooting Stars went to a **national tournament** in Salt Lake City, Utah. Teams from all over the country came to **compete**. LeBron played as hard as he could to beat the other teams.

LeBron wanted to be a
great basketball player,
like Michael Jordan (top)
and Penny Hardaway.

The Shooting Stars won first place. LeBron was named the Most Valuable Player of the tournament. The Shooting Stars later went on to win more than two hundred games.

LeBron and his teammates won many championships.

The Fab Four wanted to keep playing basketball together. So in 1999, the four friends entered Saint Vincent-Saint Mary (SVSM) High School in Akron. LeBron led the SVSM team, the "Fighting Irish," to one championship after another. In 2001, LeBron was named Ohio's "Mr. Basketball," the top high school player in the state.

Chapter 4

"King James"

During LeBron's third year at SVSM, **scouts** from the **National Basketball Association**, or NBA, came to watch him play. He was the best high school player they had ever seen. LeBron was very fast. He was very strong. And he was *very* tall: six feet, seven inches. LeBron could also jump high enough to dunk the ball through the hoop. People began calling LeBron "King James."

LeBron jumps high enough to dunk the ball down through the hoop.

LeBron about to make a jump shot in a 2003 game.

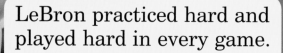

LeBron practiced hard and played hard in every game.

During his last year at SVSM, LeBron's picture was on the cover of *Sports Illustrated* magazine. He was now famous. But LeBron still worked hard at basketball practice. Every day he shot nearly eight hundred jump shots. LeBron also worked hard at his schoolwork. And he always got good grades.

LeBron graduated from high school in the spring of 2003. He was picked by the Cleveland **Cavaliers** to play on their team. Fans all across the country saw him play on TV. Wherever the Cavaliers played, crowds came to see LeBron. He was a basketball superstar.

LeBron joined the Cleveland Cavaliers pro team in 2003.

For the 2003–2004 season, LeBron was named **Rookie** of the Year, the best first-year player in the NBA. In 2004, he won a bronze medal as a member of the U.S. Olympic Basketball Team.

LeBron is one of three captains of the U.S. Men's Basketball National Team, which will compete in the 2008 Summer Olympics in Beijing, China.

LeBron holds the NBA Rookie of the Year Award.

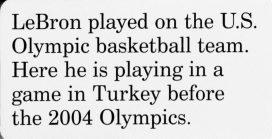

LeBron played on the U.S. Olympic basketball team. Here he is playing in a game in Turkey before the 2004 Olympics.

On December 17, 2007, LeBron became the youngest player ever to score 9,000 points! He and the Cavaliers beat the Milwaukee Bucks, 104 to 99, in double overtime.

LeBron likes to help other people. Here he is with some backpacks he is giving to Ohio schoolchildren.

LeBron uses his fame and wealth to help others, especially kids in need. He has gained the success he dreamed about. But he still pushes himself to get better. By setting such high goals for himself, LeBron has become a role model for kids everywhere.

LeBron's Own Words

"I don't need too much. Glamour and all that stuff don't excite me. I am just glad I have the game of basketball in my life."

Timeline

1984—LeBron James is born in Akron, Ohio, on December 30.

1988—LeBron receives a toy basketball set on Christmas Day.

1999—LeBron enters Saint Vincent-Saint Mary High School (SVSM) in Akron, Ohio.

2001—LeBron is named Ohio's "Mr. Basketball."

2002—LeBron appears on the cover of *Sports Illustrated* magazine.

2003—LeBron graduates from high school and is picked to play for the Cleveland Cavaliers.

2004—LeBron wins a bronze medal as a member of the U.S. Olympic Basketball Team. He is named NBA Rookie of the Year.

2006—LeBron is voted Most Valuable Player in the NBA All-Star Game.

2007—LeBron helps Cleveland defeat the Milwaukee Bucks, 104–99. He is the youngest player to score 9,000 career points.

Learn More

Books

Mattern, Joanne. *LeBron James: Young Basketball Star*. Hockessin, Del.: Mitchell Lane Publishers, 2005.

Savage, Jeff. *LeBron James*. Minneapolis, Minn.: Lerner Publications Company, 2006.

Sibila, Tom. *LeBron James: King of the Court*. Bloomington, Minn.: Red Brick Learning, 2006.

Web Sites

NBA Players: LeBron James
<http://www.nba.com/playerfile/lebron_james/bio.html>

***Time for Kids* Interview with LeBron James**
<http://www.timeforkids.com/TFK/news>

Under "Search," type in "LeBron James"; then scroll down and click on "All Eyes on LeBron James."

23

Index